ABC Ready for School
An Alphabet of Social Skills

Celeste C. Delaney

Illustrated by Stephanie Fizer Coleman

SCHOLASTIC INC.

ISBN 978-1-338-58984-9

12 11 10 9 8 7 6 5 4 3 2 1   19 20 21 22 23 24

Printed in the U.S.A.   40

First Scholastic printing, May 2019

Cover and interior design by Emily Dyer
Edited by Alison Behnke

To all the children in my life who have taught me so much—
especially my first students: Mikeah, Joseph, and Erin.

And to the teachers who helped me with ideas for preparing children for kindergarten:
Mikeah Sleigh, Erin Jennings, Kellie Cox, and Samantha Dorsch.
You do the hard work of teaching our children every day. Thank you!

A Note to Caring Adults

Starting school is an exciting time in a child's life, both for the child and for parents, teachers, and caregivers who work with the child. It can also be challenging. Transitioning from being a toddler at play to being a little person functioning in a group with the structure, rules, and expectations of preschool or kindergarten isn't always easy. There is so much to learn! Every child is born with unique strengths and weaknesses, likes and dislikes. The skills needed to do well are learned along the way: How to walk, talk, read, add, and subtract. How to share with others, embrace differences, be a good listener, and so much more.

Social skills are not just necessary for doing well in school. They are also necessary for success in life. It is up to us as adults to teach and model them. Concepts like forgiveness, perseverance, inclusion, honesty, kindness, and generosity take time to understand, but we can introduce them to young children in simple ways and foster them as children grow.

This book helps children learn essential social skills and prepare for the big step of beginning school. Each ABC picture page explores a skill, idea, or attitude that will be useful at school and in life. You can read the book from start to finish, or you can choose an individual topic you want to highlight. On pages 30–35 you will find more information about helping children get ready for school, ideas for practicing specific skills, and activities focusing on the alphabet.

I hope you will have fun exploring this book with children and being part of their learning adventure! It's an honor to share this journey with you.

—Celeste

Soon you'll be starting the big adventure of going to school.

You will learn, grow, make new friends, and have fun!

Here are some ideas to help you get ready for school.

Ask.

Raise your hand to ask your teacher a question.

Ask for help or for permission when you need it.

You can ask questions if you don't know or understand something.

Be.

Be yourself and be your best.

Always tell the truth. Be honest.

Be trustworthy. Do what you say you will do.

Cooperate.

When you cooperate, you work well with other people.

If you work in a group, listen to others. Share your ideas, too.

Help each other do something together.

Do your best.

Try hard every day.

Your work doesn't have to be perfect.

Just do the best you can.

Encourage others.

You can give courage and hope to other people.

Say "hello" to someone who is new.

Smile at someone who seems sad.

8

Follow the rules.

School has rules to help everyone be safe and happy. Rules like . . .

Listen to your teacher.

Keep your hands to yourself.

Wait to cross the street until an adult says that it is safe.

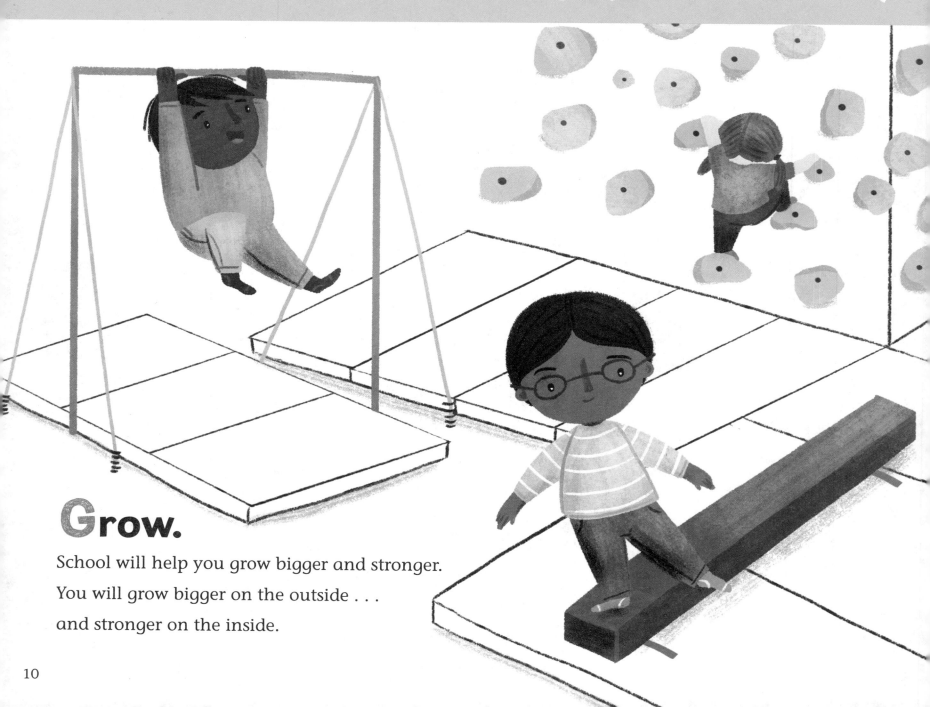

Grow.

School will help you grow bigger and stronger.

You will grow bigger on the outside . . .

and stronger on the inside.

Help everyone stay healthy.

You can help stop germs from spreading.

Wash your hands after you go to the bathroom.

Cover your mouth with your elbow when you cough or sneeze.

Include others.

Invite someone new to play with you.

Be kind to a person who is left out.

Sit next to somebody who is alone at lunchtime.

Jump!

At recess, move your body.

Jump . . . climb . . . throw . . . swing . . .

or run.

Inside, your teacher will tell you when you can dance . . .

skip . . . wiggle . . .

and wave your hands!

13

Keep learning.

You'll learn so many wonderful things at school!

Letters and words . . . numbers and counting . . .

colors and shapes . . . animals and countries . . .

and more.

Listen.

Look at the person who is talking.

Stay quiet and keep as still as you can.

That way you will hear and understand.

Move past mistakes.

You can learn from mistakes and do better next time.

Forgive others if they make mistakes.

Say "I'm sorry" if you upset someone. Help fix the problem if you can.

New things happen every day. Be brave!

Try a new game.

Play with a new toy.

Learn a new skill.

Or meet a new friend.

BUNNY
NIBBLES

Overcome.

Overcoming a challenge means learning to do something hard.

Everyone has trouble doing something.

If you keep trying, you can overcome things that are hard for you.

Play.

You will play during your days at school.

You will use your imagination and pretend.

When you play games, you can help your team.

Question.

It's good to ask questions. That's how you learn new information.

When your teacher asks you a question, give the best answer you can.

Respect others.

Be respectful by not calling people names or saying mean things.

Be kind to others when they make mistakes.

Say "please" and "thank you."

Skip, step, sing . . .
do your thing!

Spell, sketch, sew . . . now you know!

Find out what you love to do, and shine at it.

Take turns and share.

Sometimes at school, we take turns.

Wait patiently for your turn.

Share toys, books, crayons, and scissors.

They are for everyone to use.

Understand.

Understand that people are all different.

We look, dress, and talk differently.

Our families are different and we come from different places.

That is good! We can learn from each other and understand how others feel.

Volunteer.

Offer to help, even when you do not have to.

Help put away supplies. Open a door for someone.

Pick up something someone has dropped.

Work hard.

Some days, you may not want to go to school.

The work will seem hard to do at times.

Keep trying and don't give up. Work hard,

and you will learn a lot.

E**x**press yourself.

Use your words to say what is happening.

Tell an adult if you are hurt, or if someone else is hurt.

Speak up if you see someone being bullied.

You!

There is only one person like YOU! At school,

you can learn . . .

and grow . . .

and help others.

Your teacher wants to help you be the best you can be.

Zip up your jacket,

put on your shoes,

and let's go to school!

29

Getting Ready for School: Activities and Information for Teachers, Parents, and Caregivers

In many ways, kindergarten is the most important year in a child's education. It sets the stage for how children view themselves as students and how they view learning in general. If children start school well below the skill level of most of their classmates, they may feel bad about not knowing what everyone else seems to know, and they might conclude that they are not as smart as others. Without encouragement, they may begin to misbehave in class, avoid participating in difficult work, and give up on learning. On the other hand, if you are helping a child who is eager to learn and has already mastered key academic concepts, consider developing his or her abilities in areas such as art, music, or sports. Not being challenged enough can lead to boredom and misbehavior, too. And while teachers can often find these children higher level work to do, these learners may still have to work alone at times while teachers work with the other children. In these moments, students may need to rely on their self-regulation skills and other abilities. At the same time, they will be learning and strengthening social skills through working and playing with their peers. For *all* learners, kindergarten brings many valuable lessons in sharing, compassion, cooperation, and other ideas that are just as important as academic aptitude.

What Kids Need to Know Before They Go

Children naturally begin kindergarten with a wide range of abilities and readiness, both in academic knowledge and social skills. This is normal, and teachers are prepared for it. Nevertheless, the better prepared a child can be on the first day of school, the more likely it is that he or she will learn confidently and enjoy being at school. To help children prepare, parents, preschool teachers, and other caring adults can support kids as they practice and strengthen important academic and social skills *before* beginning kindergarten. The skills list on page 34 is a guideline for this practice. It reflects skills that most teachers like to see in children when they start kindergarten, and which typically make the transition to school smoother. This list will help you see areas where a child could use additional guidance before school begins. It is *not*, however, an ironclad set of requirements. If children do not have all of these abilities before starting kindergarten, it's not cause for alarm. Social and motor skills are continually evolving, and children can continue to work on skills at school and at home with the encouragement of adults. You can also download the bonus piece "My Child Isn't Ready for School. What Can I Do to Help?" at **freespirit.com/ABC** to learn other ways to provide support, such as meeting with the teacher before school starts or getting children involved in other social settings to build group social skills.

Why Are Social Skills So Important?

Social skills can be a challenge for children of all abilities. As children adjust to being in school, it's important to give these skills just as much attention as academic topics. After all, life is lived in social settings. At home, children learn to be part of a family, which includes learning skills like the importance of respecting adults, sharing toys, forgiving others, following family rules, using good manners, and playing well together.

In the broader setting of school, children will meet people they don't know. They will learn to make friends, respect others, follow directions and school rules, take turns, and share. They will also learn bigger concepts such as understanding and accepting that people come from different backgrounds and have different abilities. They will discover their own strengths and difficulties and learn about perseverance, helping others, being honest, and working hard.

As children navigate these settings and others throughout their lives, those who have developed strong social skills will experience many benefits. They will get along well with others, which in turn will help them be happier, more confident, and more eager to go to school. They'll be able to communicate their needs clearly and help others do the same. They'll be less vulnerable to bullying or peer pressure and better able to develop healthy friendships.

Gaining these skills also has other important, lasting results. Studies show that children who learn to relate well to others at a young age are less likely to drop out of school or get into other serious trouble as teenagers. As these teens grow into adults, they will carry these social skills into the workplace and community, benefiting both themselves and those around them. Positive social interactions help make life meaningful and successful. They strengthen relationships and society as a whole as people respect, understand, and help each other. So it is well worth investing time and effort into helping children learn and master these valuable skills.

Ways to Use This Book with Children

Whether you're working with one child or a group, you can use *ABC Ready for School* to spark conversation, questions, and understanding about social skills and kindergarten. The following ideas are starting points for further exploring the book and its ideas with children.

1. Let's talk about it.

Read the book together, and choose a page to talk about in more detail. To spark discussion, ask questions such as:

- What is happening in this picture?
- How do you think the people in this picture feel?
- Have you ever done what this person is doing?
- What do you think might happen next?

2. Let's find the letters.

- Talk about the letter on the page and search the picture to find objects, colors, or actions that also begin with that letter. For instance, on pages 12 and 13 (I and J), children may spot an iris, an inchworm, a pair of jeans, and a jump rope. On page 5 (B), children may point out a bow, buttons, drawings of a bird and bear, the color blue, and a pair of best friends.

- Ask children what other school-related words start with the letter. You can make suggestions if they have trouble getting started. For example, L is for *listen* in the book, but it could also be for *laugh*, *learn*, or even *lunch*.

3. Let's draw.

- Choose a skill or an idea from the book and have children draw pictures of how it could look or be used in school and elsewhere.

- Have one large piece of paper or a large cardboard box that children can all draw on to complete a project together. This group activity involves a lot of cooperation, turn taking, patience, and sharing. In addition, it requires children to accept the fact that others may not carry out the task exactly the way they think it should be done.

- Trace each child's outline onto a separate large piece of paper, writing the child's name at the top or bottom. Then go around the group asking children to say what they like about each child, and write those words inside that child's outline, leaving the face area blank. Have each child complete his or her own portrait by adding facial features and hair.

4. Let's play a game.

- Play a board game or ball game that involves having to take turns and wait patiently between turns.

- Make any competitive game into a cooperative game by having children work together to achieve a goal instead of competing with each other to win. For example, in a board game, you could place just one piece on the board and have everyone take turns rolling the die and moving the piece to see how quickly they can get to the end as a group. Or children could cooperate to see how many times they can get a ball through a hoop or into a goal.

- Play a game that requires children to communicate with each other. For example, you could attach a picture of a recognizable person or character to each child's forehead or back. Each child then has to ask others yes/no questions to figure out who the picture is of. (For example, "Is it a cartoon character?")

5. Let's pretend.

Role playing is a good way to practice social skills. Try having your group act out the following scenes and situations, or others that you think of:

- Talk about a social skill from the book (such as *encourage*) and have a group of children act out how that skill might look in action.

- Ask one child to tell you a story about something he or she has done or is interested in. While the child is talking, demonstrate poor listening skills—looking anywhere but at him or her, fiddling with something, and so on. Afterward, ask the child how that felt. As a group, talk about the importance of giving your attention to the person who is talking so he or she knows you are listening.

- Ask one child in the group to act out an emotion and have the others try to guess what feeling he or she is showing.

Additional Information

For more helpful information about kindergarten readiness, visit **freespirit.com/ABC**. You'll find two documents to download, print, or share. They contain additional tips for families and other caring adults to help young children get ready for school.

"Helping Your Child Succeed in School"
This list of ideas contains practical ways for parents or caregivers to help children make the most of their learning time at school.

"My Child Isn't Ready for School. What Can I Do to Help?"
Not every child is ready for school at the same time. This document shares simple ways to help children get ready at their own pace.

Skills for Kindergarten Readiness

These skills are all helpful as young children enter kindergarten. Talk and work with each child in your care to build and strengthen these skills and prepare every child to have a great start to school. For easy reference, you can make a copy of this list (or download it at freespirit.com/ABC) and make note of which skills the child has mastered, and which ones could still use improvement.

Name: _____

Most of the time and without help, the child can . . .

- identify all the letters of the alphabet out of order.
- identify numbers 1 through 10 out of order.
- name and draw three basic shapes: circle, square, and cross.
- write his or her name.
- name 6 or more colors accurately.
- use child-safe scissors to cut across an 8-inch page.
- sit quietly and calmly while someone is reading or talking for 10 minutes.
- follow verbal instructions consistently.
- work independently on an assigned project for 10 minutes.
- go to the bathroom independently.
- eat independently.
- separate from a parent or caregiver without significant anxiety.
- take off and put on shoes independently.
- take turns in a simple game with others.
- share toys without getting upset.

About the Author and Illustrator

Celeste C. Delaney grew up in New Zealand, where much of life is lived outdoors. As a child she loved playing at the beach, reading, playing piano, writing stories, and drawing. She left New Zealand after earning a degree in occupational therapy and has since lived and worked in many countries including the United States, India, Malaysia, China, and Mexico. Celeste enjoys traveling, teaching, art projects, and writing. She works as an occupational therapist with children, which challenges her to be patient and flexible, and rewards her with smiles, hugs, and the joy of seeing children grow and learn. Celeste lives near Portland, Oregon, with her husband Chris. They have three grown children, two sons-in-law, and one granddaughter.

Stephanie Fizer Coleman is an illustrator and designer whose love of nature inspires much of her art. After getting a degree in history, she found her true passion in illustration. She enjoys experimenting with patterns, textures, and brilliant colors in her work. Stephanie lives in West Virginia with her husband and two silly dogs. When she's not drawing, she can be found puttering around the garden, trying out new vegan recipes in the kitchen, or curled up with a good book and a cup of tea.